Contents

You are the Ultimate Infinite Existence

Through the knowledge of the Supreme Existence, man becomes the Infinite Supreme Consciousness.

– Yoga Vashista

PORLA LINGAPPA

Foreword

Thath thwam asi (You are the ultimate infinite consciousness)

– Vedas

Oh! Ramachandra! "As metal is refined in the furnace, so man unifies himself with and becomes the Infinite Divine consciousness (Supreme Self/ *Paramatma*) by acquiring the knowledge of the Infinite consciousness."

– Sri Vasishta Gita

"Only the young, the strong, and the people with sharp intelligence can see the Supreme Consciousness."

– Upanishads

In the process of evolution of knowledge,Indian philosophers have gone beyond the concepts of various gods and discovered the infinite Supreme conciousness/Soul present here and recognized that we are also a part of it, attained ultimate freedom and experienced the priceless bliss of Brahman that comes with it, which is the greatest gift of knowledge that Indians gave to the world thousands of years ago.

The prominent 19th-century German philosopher Arthur Schopenhauer, greatly influenced by the Upanishads, called them "the highest product of human wisdom" and stated that "in the whole world, there is nothing so beneficial and sublime as the study of the Upanishads."

Upanishad means "sitting with someone". It means a conversation between a guru and a disciple on spiritual matters. Dissatisfied with the elaborate rituals, there are discussions on spiritual matters such as karma, soul, and the Supreme Soul, and discussions on the paths of devotional knowledge. Spiritual knowledge is the Vedanta in the Upanishads. Kshatriyas and well-educated women used to participate in the discussions.

Since these Upanishads are in the last part of the Vedas, the philosophical knowledge in them is called Vedanta. The Upanishads propound the Advaita doctrine. The link between Sharp intelligence and Seeing God, infinite Substratum, or Supreme Consciousness is only told by ancient Indian philosophy, and no other philosophy or religion in the world has addressed this unique and interesting subject.

Also, Indian philosophers advised us to be spiritually free, not just spiritual.

The value of spiritual freedom that comes from transcendental knowledge is indescribable.

Indeed, there is no greater benefit in the world for human life than freedom. It is for this freedom that every living being and every thing in creation yearns and strives, says Swami Vivekananda.

> The whole of Indian philosophy is centred on the realization of the Supreme Being. Man must become divine by realizing the Divine. Idols or temples or churches or books are only a support and help in his spiritual childhood and they are the stepping stones for his progress."
>
> – Swami Vivekananda

> "You are the Ultimate Infinite Existence; nothing is beyond, above, or other than you in the Universe."
>
> – Vedhantha

Recognising and seeing your infinite existence in the outside universe and within you and constantly experiencing this great reality whose essential nature is peaceful and blissful is the great revolutionary and ultimate philosophical discovery made by the ancient Indian philosophy called Vedanta.

"By being pleasant and smiling always, it takes you nearer to God than any prayer"

— Swamy Vivekananda

This knowledge of the Infinite Consciousness or the Supreme Soul is called *Brahma gnana* or Vedanta.

Upanishads, Sri Bhagavad Gita, Sri Vasishta Gita, Avaduta Gita, Ashtavakra Gita, etc., are the true scriptures that teach Brahma gnana.

Human life is a mixture of happiness and sorrow. When happiness comes, a man is happy. But when sorrow comes, a man cannot bear it and becomes depressed. Knowledge of the Infinite Consciousness/Supreme Soul is necessary to easily overcome such sorrow, accept happiness and sorrow with equanimity, and move forward in life.

This equanimity is what our ancestors/Indian philosophers called "*Sthita Pragna.*" After fulfilling all family responsibilities, a person feels that the journey of life has come to an end. The question of what has to be done next begins. At such a stage of life, only transcendental knowledge can show the direction and enable the journey of life to continue with eternal enthusiasm. In light of today's modern science, it is not a difficult task for intellectuals who are knowledgeable in modern science to acquire knowledge that creates such a great state of mind. The ocean of ignorance, which is difficult to cross, has been crossed by wise people in just a minute by the ship called *Gnana yukti* means Knowledge + Cleverness – Sri Vashista Gita. Especially modern sciences such as physics and astronomy have almost reached this state of Brahman *gnana*/Darshan/vision. That is, they have concluded that this infinite universe is sustained by a single entity.

The Nobel Prize in Physics was awarded to three physicists in 2022 for proving that this universe is not the absolute truth as it appears to us.

Swamy Vivekananda had said this earlier.

"Science is nothing but the finding of unity."

"As soon as science would reach perfect unity, it would stop from further progress because it would reach the goal. Thus, chemistry could not progress further when it discovered one element out of which all others could be made. Physics would stop when it would be able to fulfil its services in discovering one energy of which all the others are but manifestations. The science of religion becomes perfect when it discovers Him who is the one life in a universe of death, Him who is the constant basis of an ever-changing world, and One who is the only Soul of which all souls are but delusive manifestations. Thus, is it, through multiplicity and duality, that the ultimate unity is reached."

Religion can go no further.

This is the goal of all science.

All science is bound to come to this conclusion in the long run. Manifestation, and not creation, is the word of science today, and the Hindu is only glad that what he has been cherishing in his bosom for ages is going to be taught in a more forcible language and with further light from the latest conclusions of science"

– Swamy Vivekananda

Swami Vivekananda advised combining Western technology and Indian spiritualism for the well-being and progress of society.

Creation, God, the goal of human life, etc. are not much discussed in our schools/education systems. That is why people go to temples and gurus, and through other processes, they try to gain this knowledge and spiritual freedom. However, some fake gurus deceive this opportunity with false knowledge. For the common man, the knowledge of God is very difficult and mysterious. Ancient Indian philosophers proclaimed that after thousands of years of research, we can see the Supreme Soul/Infinite consciousness through the knowledge of Infinite Consciousness/Ultimate Existence called "Paramartha gnana"

Therefore, those who are interested in this knowledge should first study these scriptures. If they do not understand it by then, they can take advice from a proper guru. Because for some wise people, this knowledge is very easily understood by their own wisdom.

"The knowledge of Brahman/Infinite consciousness is achieved by studying spiritual scriptures, meditation, faith in the guru's words, and wisdom, or by wisdom alone."

– Sri Vasishta Gita

Similarly, according to me, this generation of wise people understands this knowledge very quickly.

If we look at the latest discoveries in astronomy, we will find a surprising thing. That is, an astronomer named Hubble discovered that the universe is expanding. The expansion of the universe is happening very rapidly. Scientists say that the reason for this expansion is 68 percent dark energy and that there is also 27 percent dark matter in the universe. Scientists say that the dark energy, which is a high percentage, is a characteristic of the sky. The universe that we see is only 5 percent. That is, in reality, the universe is also filled with unity, whether it is a single substance or an entity.

The vision of such a unified infinite universe by Indian philosophers is a revolutionary discovery with great intellectual wealth. Today's quantum physics also suggests that matter is another form of the infinite quantum field. It has come to the conclusion that matter is only one manifestation of the infinite universe, but not a separate entity. Similarly, energy is also just a form of matter.

The vision of such a unified infinite universe by Indian philosophers thousands of years ago was a revolutionary discovery with great intellectual acumen. Today's quantum physics also says this. The research of our ancestors was about what this universe is and where it came from. Where did we come from? What will happen in the end? What is our duty? The process of finding the answer to the questions is the research that discovered the secret of this creation, which the Advaita philosophy in the Vedas is the main one that reveals those secrets of infinite existence. When it comes to technology, the discoveries of zero (0) and iron/steel, etc., discovered by Indians have contributed a lot to today's scientific and technological progress.

Indian philosophy is the education that shows the true position, status, true form of man and his relationship with this infinite universe. This is also called *Paravidya*. This is also called spiritual education, *Paramartha/Paramathma gnana*. Our ancestors, who knew that their true form was infinite existence, experienced great joy. They called this Brahmanandam/Supreme Bliss. They wrote books of this knowledge so that future generations could also know and experience this Brahmanandam/Supreme Bliss. These are the Vedas, Upanishads, Mahabharata, Bhagavad Gita, Avadata Gita, Vasishta Gita Ashtavakra Gita etc.

This stage of Vedanta knowledge took place in India thousands of years ago. People from all walks of life played a role in this search for knowledge.

"All the Upanishads were compiled by Kshatriyas."

— Swami Vivekananda

Most of the sages who wrote the Upanishads are unknown. Swamy Vivekananda comments, "The highest men in society are always calm, silent, and unknown."

This type of situation can be seen in the present time, too, in scientific inventions. For example, very few know the inventor of the electric bulb, Thomas Alva Edison, but know about brand names and the companies which manufacture electric bulbs. Similarly, alternating current (AC) and the AC motor were invented by a genius scientist called Nikola Tesla. Very few know him, but many people know about the companies which manufacture AC electrical equipment and AC electric motors.

So, most of people know about the commentators of Vedanta/Brahmagyana like Sri Krishna, Sage Vashista, Dattatreya Avadhuta, Ashtavakra, Adi Shankara, and so many other great commentators and preachers of Vedanta but don't know the actual inventors of this great philosophy which revolutionised human ideas about God, the creator, and revealed his true nature. It took them to the highest level, the ultimate abode of God, and to the highest ultimate Divine being, the Paramatman himself, identifying man with the Highest Infinite Existence here.

Recognizing and seeing your infinite presence in the external universe and within yourself and constantly experiencing this great reality that is peaceful and joyful is the great revolutionary and ultimate philosophical discovery made by the ancient Indian philosophy called Vedanta.

Although the knowledge of Brahman was discovered in India thousands of years ago, it is a matter of concern that a large number of people are engaged in idol worship even today. A person who has attained Brahman/Supreme knowledge about our existence is not at this stage of spiritual initiation as stated in the Upanishads, A person who has attained physical freedom, mental freedom, and spiritual freedom, and basks in the bliss of Brahman, does not indulge in the secondary spiritual activities that are fraught with fear, which are the initial stage of noble evolution. This freedom does not mean complete renunciation of all worldly pleasures. More than all these, they say that there is great happiness, which is obtained only through the supreme knowledge/Brahman knowledge/vision of the ultimate infinite Consciousness. Their intention is that the future generations should also obtain the supreme happiness that they experienced through the attainment of this knowledge. That is why the Vedas, the Upanishads called Vedanta, have been written as scriptures by various sages who considered this knowledge essential for attaining Bliss in mankind. The Bhagavad Gita says that "I have created four varnas based on the division of merit and inherent nature of people, but some selfish people have considered this as based on heridatory and have destroyed Indian society and made our country fall into the hands of foreign invaders who are less developed than us in every way."

> The Indian caste system, based on hereditary division of labor, is a decisive impediment to the power and progress of India
>
> – Karl Marx

It is true that the spread of this knowledge was hindered by the caste system prevalent in India for ages, which caused weakness and natural division due to which the foreign invaders could easily enslave India for hundreds of years. According to Swami Vivekananda, the Vedas teach equality and are against the caste system of inequality that is practised today. Modern scientists and intellectuals of Western countries are studying the Upanishads and Brahman knowledge texts more than present-day Indians. Especially in Germany, they have been studying the Upanishads for a few hundred years. In India, only a few know about these scriptures. Most of today's educated people have not even read the important 8-10 Upanishads. This is an unfortunate situation.

In fact, we as Indians should be very proud of the great heritage of knowledge, but the efforts made by those who claim to be the rightful owners of today's Vedanta education to spread this knowledge are only nominal. Those who enjoy worldly pleasures with a business perspective in the name of this spiritual education are also causing a lot of damage to the spread of this knowledge. Such a great heritage of knowledge is not found in any other religion except in Vedanta; no other religion speaks of the "Sight of the Supreme Soul/Infinite consciousness"; it is a stage they have not yet reached. Indians crossed such stages thousands of years ago and saw the Infinite Supreme Consciousness/soul here and proclaimed it to the world. Karl Marx also said that all world religions originated from India.

In this infinite universe, we see many things and events in creation endlessly. Our goal is to see the relationship between them and the ultimate meaning of creation, our life and its aim, and our existence in this infinite consciousness, which is the source of all these. The causes and results of many events are constantly being discovered by the fields of science and technology and used for the welfare of humanity. After conquering material nature and fulfilling the essential needs, with the search for knowledge related to the true nature of human existence, we call this knowledge Brahman gnana or Vedanta acquired. Veda means knowledge. The word Vidya is also derived from the word Veda. Vedas mean books of knowledge. These were compiled for the first time by Veda Vyasa Maharishi.

I tried to correlate developments in modern theoretical Physics, Chemistry, Astrophysics, Neurology, etc., with Vedantic philosophy, also called Brahma jnana.

I deeply believe that by diligently studying the ultimate knowledge in this book and adding wisdom, this generation of wise people will definitely have the darshan/sight of the Supreme Consciousness/Soul.

My entire endeavour is to introduce today's educated people to this transcendental knowledge of Ultimate Existence, which gives peace of mind, happiness, continuous experience of Bliss, and the ability to function more effectively and efficiently without much tiredness in the daily activities of life.

Porla Lingappa

+918333011000

Email – plingappa@gmail.com

Knowledge of Infinite Divine/Ultimate Consciousness (Paramartha Gnanam)

After the emergence of man on earth, man started acquiring knowledge. Initially, he conquered nature and provided food, security, and other necessities for his life. After these needs were met, another question remained for man. That is, how and where did this creation come about? Is there a creator/God for this? If so, what are the characteristics of the creator/God? What are our duties, and what is the righteous path in life? What happens to us after death? Is there life after death, and is there rebirth? Questions like this started to arise. In search of answers to these questions, the ancient Indians found the answers much earlier and visited the Supreme Divine consciousness/Soul/ God. The science behind these answers is called Vedanta. This research has been conducted here for several thousand years. The climatic conditions here in India also helped a lot in acquiring this knowledge.

To understand Paramartha Gyanam/Knowledge of Ultimate Infinite Divine Existence, one has to focus on the infinite universe here from the limited worldly knowledge/ observations. One has to view the infinite universe with the power of imagination/eye of knowledge. The observations of the limited world we constantly encounter and the results that come from them are insufficient. The instruments and methods of measuring our finite world are not sufficient to understand the properties and nature of the infinite universe here. The infinite truth has to be perceived as it is. That requires a lot of intelligence, philosophy, and intellectual courage to accept new things. As science progresses, many such incidents have confused scientists. For example, when it was discovered that the earth is round, there was opposition from the then flat-bed theory. When it was said that the earth is not the centre of this universe, there was a similar opposition from the orthodoxy. This situation prevailed from the physical theories up to modern quantum theories. We can also observe a similar situation in science.

Let us now try to see the infinite non-dual existence by studying the microscopic world.

When we observe the atom, the atom and the microscopic factors such as electrons, protons, and neutrons, and even the further microscopic factors such as quarks, a new thing comes into experience. That is, different atoms are formed only by the difference in their numbers, e.g., Oxygen has eight electrons, protons, and neutrons, and Nitrogen has seven electrons, neutrons, and protons, etc. But electrons, protons, and neutrons are the same uniform in all atoms.

One thing that we understand so far is that this visible universe is formed by factors/particles smaller than atoms.

Now, let's study the relationship between the fundamental particles and energy and space, which look like different entities.

If we go further, the great physicist Einstein proved that matter and energy are the same with his famous equation $E=mc^2$.

Now, the sky appears to be different from energy and matter. According to the Vedanta of Indian philosophers, the infinite entity is theorised as having different forms of one infinite existence without any division into the five elements called fire, air, water, earth and sky. The sky is not separate from energy and matter, but all are just manifestations of one Infinite Existence. According to quantum physics, if we look deeply into the matter, it exists not as particles but as waves. If we look even deeper, string theory says that waves are also absorbed in the sky. When we observe the connection between energy and matter in the sky, we immediately understand that this sky is not empty space and is separate from matter and energy; they are the same in this Infinite Existence.

"I regard consciousness as fundamental. I regard matter as derivative from consciousness." – Max Planck, a physicist who paved the way for quantum physics.

Now let us try to view infinite existence from the perspective of the macrocosm, that is, the infinite universe. Once we turn our attention to the infinite universe, we see the planet Earth, the star called the Sun, and countless stars at night. All of these are in their specific positions and are in continuous rotation. If we look at it through a telescope, we also see galaxies. Our solar system is part of the Milky Way galaxy, and there is a black hole in the center of the Milky Way. All the stars and planets in the galaxy are rotating around it.

The sky that holds all of these in fixed orbits is visible. The sky that holds such a huge number of planets made of matter must have a stronger and more stable proposition than all of these. If we think about it with a simple astronomical perspective, we understand that now according to quantum field science, the sky, planets, stars, and galaxies, which are all made of matter, are infinitely spread out and have an infinite proposition that is beyond our imagination, and that is what this matter is. All the planets have arisen and are actually only one state of that infinite proposition and appear in this way to our limited observation. In fact, the infinite existence here has this kind of active nature by itself. This infinite universe is always active except in a state of decay. This visible universe made of visible matter is not different from the infinite universe. When there is only one entity infinitely, then the existence of another second object here is not possible. When there is infinity, there must be only one object. The Indian philosophers who have reached this state called it infinite pure consciousness, which is what is called Infinite Consciousness in English. This pure consciousness is beyond the invisible universe. If we want to know its complete true form, our sensory knowledge is not enough, that is, we cannot see it with our logical tools or physical experiments. We can experience it to some extent with extrasensory knowledge, that is, with the power of imagination. Understanding the infinite pure consciousness in our limited world is a process of seeing this pure consciousness in another way. For this, we need to focus on reaching the deepest state or state within ourselves, which can be reached through meditation or knowledge. In such a still, peaceful and blissful state, we can directly see the supreme state of infinite pure consciousness, which is called the Supreme Being. This process can be said to be a great revolutionary peak of knowledge experiment discovered by Indian philosophers.

Our philosophers do not say to give up the basic pleasures of food, drink, or sex with women/men. They say that there is another great pleasure/bliss in this life that is beyond all these and obtained through the knowledge of the Supreme Existence. Therefore, they desire that everyone should attain this blissful knowledge as much as possible, and after having the vision of infinite consciousness, there will be no limits to his happiness. Interest in all worldly pleasures and pleasures diminishes.

"One who has seen the infinite Supreme Divine Consciousness/Soul for a moment does not show interest in worldly activities, similar to one who has seen heaven does not show interest in the graveyard"

– Vashista Geeta

But he, too, can do things without any desire. This can be understood if we observe the words spoken by the child-yogi/sage Dhruv during the period of his penance as a result of his realisation/Appearance of Vishnu. "I have done penance for worldly pleasures like a kingdom, but I have been blessed with your Vision/Appearance/darshan like finding a diamond while searching for a piece of glass. I have no desire to ask for any other boon."

This is the best example of how a man loses much interest in worldly pleasure after attaining the Supreme knowledge, i.e., the Vision of Divine Supreme Consciousness/God. The great children of wisdom we see in the history of Indian Vedanta are Nachiketa, Dhruva, Prahlad, and Ashtavakra.

Swami Vivekananda has said this about how to live life after gaining Vedanta knowledge.

"This world is a great gymnasium in which we play, and our life is an eternal holiday" is a statement that gives great comfort to the mind just by listening to it. How fortunate are those who live their lives practising this in real life? This application to our life is said from the knowledge of the Supreme. This existence called the infinite Supreme Soul/Consciousness here is doing these events of creation, manifestation and destruction like a game, like a play, for an infinite time without any results/adding or losing anything. When this Paramartha/Paramatma/Infinite Consciousness knowledge is understood, we can naturally live life in this way as an eternal holiday, like a play.

"Relate thyself not with the future, nor with what has gone by; live the present out with a smiling heart"

– Vashista Geetha

Vedanta knowledge is completely opposed to superstitions and blind beliefs. Because the knowledge gained as a result of many thousands of years of research is very scientific. It is said in the Vashita Gita, "Whoever abandons the conscious efforts of man and believes that some unseen force inspires him should be renounced and driven away." This verse shows how unequivocally our sages have condemned superstitions. There is a very surprising conversation in the Sri Ramayana. It is a conversation between Sri Rama and Lakshmana. When Sri Dasharatha, father of Rama, ordered Sri Rama to go to the forest for 14 years after leaving the throne, Lakshmana got angry and said this: "To order a son who is worthy of a kingdom to go to the forest in this way means that the king has lost his mind. Therefore, such a king, be he his father or anyone else, maybe ultimately Lord Brahma, the creator himself, should be removed from that position immediately, and you should ascend the throne. If you order, I will take action against our father right now." Hearing these words, Shri Ram says that he should not do that. Let us consider this as our destiny and obey our Father's order. Then Lakshmana replies in this way again: "The word destiny should not come from the mouth of a wise man. If you believe in fate, why are your wide arms, why are your spiritual knowledge and why are your powerful bow and arrows?"

That is, a wise man should never practice the superstitious and ignorant way of thinking about fate. There is a very good and profound Vedic message in this conversation. But in today's time, many people do not care much about it. If you notice, in many instances, Lakshmana considers his life insignificant and goes to war. This is a characteristic of a person with true Vedic knowledge.

Similarly, as part of the search for God, people constantly go on pilgrimages to worship idols. Sri Ramakrishna Paramahansa was saddened to see even old people going to temples. Swami Vivekananda established an "Advaitha Ashram" in the Himalayas and did not allow any idol worship there.

Finally, he did not even agree to keep the portrait of his guru Sri Ramakrishna Paramahansa there. All the publications related to the Ramakrishna Math come out from there.

This transcendental knowledge is perfect. It is not an "ideology" that is against today's materialistic philosophy. It is a knowledge that completes materialism. Seeing the peaceful nature within us and being happy is not a matter/ science that is against any other socio-political theory. It is a personal matter. However, it is not easy to understand this knowledge without having enough wealth to travel through life. Sri Swami Vivekananda says that teaching Vedanta Philosophy to those who are starving is an insult to humanity. In ancient times, kings and emperors only contributed a lot to the attainment of this knowledge or its propagation. Others completely left the household life and took up the monastic life and dedicated themselves to the attainment of this knowledge. Whether it is a *sanyasi* (Monastic) or *Sansari* (household) ashram to choose is a personal matter. One who is immersed in worldly matters, and the best of these is to attain the state of knowledge by practising the process of Karma Yoga/working without attachments to the results of work is mentioned in the Bhagavad Gita.

When it comes to the attainment of transcendental knowledge, attaining the state of knowledge depends on one's intellectual power. The Upanishads say that only the young, the strong, and the intelligent can see the Supreme Divine Consciousness/Soul/*Paramatma darshan*. Only Indian philosophy speaks of the great state of consciousness called the vision of the Supreme Consciousness Self. That, too, is due to intellectual power: "The transcendental knowledge is attained only by the friend called intellect who is well-versed in imagination and scepticism but not by any other process."

"Half of ignorance is destroyed by free exchange of thought; half of the remainder is dispelled by application to philosophy, the rest fades away The Light of SelfReflection"

"Liberation is not on the other side of the sky, nor In the netherworld, nor on earth; liberation lies in the mind purified by proper knowing"

– Vashista Geetha

"There is no other path to liberation than knowledge of the Ultimate Supreme Consciousness"

– Vashista Gita

The constant contemplation of the pure Supreme Consciousness in the mind is called "great worship" and "great meditation"

– Sri Vasishta Gita

Swami Vivekananda says that two types of people do not have desires: the wise and the idiot. The wise person naturally loses all desires due to his knowledge of the Supreme/infinite Philosophy and does not have any desires. In such a state, he experiences a lot of Brahmananda/Bliss and appears somewhat different in society. The famous Vashista Gita speaks about the happiness that this state of knowledge gives.

Oh Ramachandra! "The despair that arises from the realisation of knowledge of Supreme Infinite Consciousness brings so much happiness to the mind greater than a kingdom, than the moon, than the best of the spring season, than the best of the mating." - Sri Vasishta Gita

"Like a drunkard, the wise, experiencing the bliss of Brahman, are free from the fear of rebirth and do not remember the (Karma) activities done or the (Karma) activities not done."

In ancient times, in our country (in India), such Vedanta education was taught in the *Gurukulas*/Education institutes at the early stage of childhood. Sri Krishna received such knowledge in the Ashram of Sandipani and Sri Rama through the teachings of Vasishta at a young age, and by practising it in life, they became such great sages and guides/Avatars/incarnations. Unfortunately, in our current times, this education is not being taught along with otherworldly education. That is why the mental state of the people in society is not right, and even highly educated people are getting confused due to a lack of clarity about our existence. Due to their ignorance, they lack love and sympathy for society and become addicted to alcohol and other intoxicants. They are trying to find peace in such things. But such practices and habits do not give permanent peace and happiness. Only the knowledge of the Supreme Infinite Consciousness/Supreme Soul/Ultimate reality can give man permanent happiness and joy.

There is no object in this world that gives permanent immense pleasure and happiness other than the Knowledge of Infinite Supreme Consciousness.

How to live after attaining the state of supreme knowledge or salvation is explained in the Vasishta Gita.

"Oh Rama, having attained this supreme knowledge/state of salvation, drink, wander and enjoy this world with women in a playful manner"

– Sri Vasishta Gita

The liberated man thinketh ever upon that Being who is the goal of all philosophical reasoning, who is the conviction of every ; who is the All; who is Everywhere; who is Everything

– Vasista Geetha

"Those who know the essence of suffering have spoken of Doubt as the greatest sorrow," Sri Vasishta Gita.

Here doubt means doubts about the existence of the Supreme Consciousness and the existence of life and death, about the existence of God and about the relationship between man and Supreme consciousness. This doubt is removed by gaining knowledge of the infinite Supreme Consciousness, the origin and dissolution of this universe, which is the source of its existence. This is also called infinite pure consciousness. The relationship of man to all these, the issue of heaven and hell, and the doubts about sins and virtues and the highest duties of human birth, etc., can be crossed by wise people in just a minute by the ship called "Gnana yukti" (Combination of knowledge of Supreme consciousness with cleverness)

– Sri Vasishta Gita

In previous times, some foreigners came to India and learned this knowledge, went to their places, preached it, and became famous as great sages because this knowledge answered the questions related to creation and the existence of man.

Modern Science - Vedantha

Currently, modern science is only one step away from reaching its ultimate goal, which is the Grand Unification of all the forces and matter and everything that exists here in the infinite universe. Physics has almost proven that this entire universe is one infinite and unbroken entity. Quantum physics and astronomical research today talk about dark matter and dark energy. It is being proven that all this is nothing, but the manifestations of a single infinite entity as stated in Vedanta. This is what the Vedas have proclaimed as "Jagat Midya Brahma Satya" (Infinite Consciousness is real, Finite Visible world is not real).

Jagat Midya does not mean that this visible universe does not exist. The visible universe, what we see, is not complete reality; it is partial reality. The five elements, Earth, water, air, fire, and space, are not independent. They are all interconnected and manifestations of the same Infinite Existence. Ultimately, there is no second object in this universe, whether seen from the perspective of the microcosm or from the perspective of the macrocosm. Ultimately, matter, energy, and space are not separate or limited. There is only one entity that is infinitely unbroken, which is this manifestation called creation, manifestation, and destruction, which is happening like a play. This infinite entity is the Supreme conscious/Self/Soul, and when applied to us, it is said to be the Individual Self/soul. Once our thinking goes from the concept of a limited universe to the concept of an infinite universe, our entire way of thinking changes and the meaning of this visible universe and our existence and life changes, and a great light appears in us.

After everything in life is enjoyed - food, drink, and the happy confluence of male or female - there remains a desire. It is a kind of dissatisfaction, a great doubt that causes sorrow. By resolving this doubt, the human being yearns for the greatest peace and happiness that can be obtained. The knowledge of the Supreme Consciousness/Being alone dispels the doubt in life and brings unlimited joy to the mind.

The first thing to focus on in this path of knowledge is that we must turn our attention away from our daily finite world of existence and understand that the creation or existence here is infinite. Similarly, the stars, galaxies, planets, and the sky are all seen to be moving in specific places in this infinite universe. As Lord Krishna says in the Gita, "This entire world is like a garland of flowers that have been planted in Me."

It is understood that the sky, where such gigantic stars and planets have a fixed position in a specific place, is not empty. As Sri Vasishta says, "Like waves in water, like clay in the pot, this visible world is in this infinite Supreme Consciousness/Self/Soul. How can this Supreme Self/Soul be emptiness."

"Like waves in water, the infinite Supreme Consciousness/Self/Soul experiences the state of creation of the visible Universe and its dissolution within itself."

In this way, while contemplating the infinite external universe, we should also look within ourselves. For this, sometimes meditation is needed. Through meditation, we finally reach the deepest state within ourselves. It is said about this in the Bhagavad Gita. "The senses are superior to the physical body, the mind is superior to the senses. Beyond the mind is the intellect. Beyond the intellect, within/above it, the Supreme Consciousness/Paramatma is in our body." Its nature is peaceful and joyful/blissful. If we can reach and experience this state of the Supreme Soul, a great peace and happiness will immediately arise. This ultimate state of peace and bliss within us is the true nature of the infinite Supreme Being/Consciousness.

That is, there is only one infinite being here. This infinite being has been called by different names by different philosophers.

"*Ekam sat vipra bahuda vadhanti*" - Rigveda. It means that One infinite being is called by different names by wise men.

"This infinite Supreme consciousness is called Nothing/Emptiness by nullifiers, Time by the time-worn, Brahman by Vedantins, and God by the God-worn."

– Sri Vasishta Gita

Whatever exists in this infinite consciousness is the ultimate reality; nothing exists beyond or above this existence; it is final.

Similarly, we are also nothing but this ultimate reality.

It is a wonderful and astonishing experience within us when we realise this great truth about our true nature and existence here.

In the Bhagavad Gita, Lord Krishna says that our eyes are not enough to see his universal form; we need the eye of knowledge. The eye of knowledge means imagination. "The imagination is more important than knowledge," says the great physicist Albert Einstein. His theory of relativity revolutionised and took the previous knowledge of physics to another level and said that time and space are not specific in themselves; they change depending on the position of the person observing it. That is, if we travel close to the speed of light, the speed of time slows down. If we look at a moving object from a fixed position, it has a speed. Similarly, if we also travel with it, its speed slows down according to our measurements. If we can travel at the same speed as it, its speed will be zero. That is, its speed is the same as before;

the only difference is that the position in which we measure it has changed, so we will observe that its speed has also changed. So, this universe that we see is relatively real. What we see is not the complete truth. That is, today's physics and other sciences, such as chemistry, have discovered that the entire universe that we see is not the absolute truth. Here, the results of two experiments in particular have been something different from our existing knowledge of physics. The surprising thing that was discovered in the double-slit experiment is that particles, such as electrons, are visible as particles only when someone is observing them. When no one observes them, they are in the form of waves. This astonishing fact is something that science has not yet understood.

In this way, recent medical research has almost discovered that our individual consciousness is inextricably linked to this infinite cosmic consciousness. "In quantum physics, a particle does not exist as classical physics observes. It does not exist in a definite physical position. Instead, it is a cloud of probabilities. If the measuring instrument, as it observes it, comes into contact with its environment, the particle loses its "superposition" of multiple states. It collapses into a specific, measurable state. Penrose hypothesised that "every time the quantum-wave function collapses in the brain in this way, it leads to an experience of consciousness."

If this quantum theory of consciousness, involving microtubules in the brain, is correct, it would revolutionise our understanding of consciousness and would also support the trailblazing theory that consciousness, at the quantum level, can be everywhere at once. In other words, it would be everywhere at once, suggesting that your own consciousness could be hypothetically connected to quantum particles beyond your brain, perhaps connected to Infinite Consciousness."

In a similar way, two entangled particles can communicate instantaneously faster than the speed of light, no matter how far apart they are positioned in the universe.

The above experimental results tell us a great thing. That is, in this infinite universe, the sky/space matter and energy do not exist separately. There is no distance or separation between all of these. This entire universe is unbroken infinitely and is one single object or entity. There is no other second object, which is what we call Advaita Paramatma/ one Infinite Consciousness. *"Ekameva Advitiyam Brahma"* means that there is no other second object in this universe. This is an object that is infinitely unbroken and is called "pure consciousness." The rest of the visible world is visible in various ways only through the observational field. For example, we can only see light, through which this universe appears to us as limited by the reflection of light.

If we can see the same X-rays or infrared rays, this entire visible world will appear in a different way. Similarly, many radio waves in the world and many waves from this universe are transmitted and pass through our brains every moment, but we cannot perceive them; only the receptors related to them can perceive. Similarly, we can't see the air which contains oxygen, which is an essential life-supporting element. That is, the visible world that we see is only a part of the universe. It means that we cannot see the entire form of this universe completely with our senses.

If we take a summary from all the above things with a transcendental perspective, what we understand is that what is here is infinite and unbroken Existence including the forms of matter, space, and energy that we see. We also have that transcendental essence or say element in us, so when we understand this, a light shines within us and our entire thinking process changes, and we get eternal peace and happiness that cannot be described in words. This realisation is called Liberation or Moksha or *Kaivalyapadam or Parandamam or Paramapadam or Paramatma Darshanam.* The great achievement of our Vedantic knowledge is to experience life as a great blessing, enjoying the peace and happiness that this knowledge brings. The bliss of knowledge of Infinite Consciousness/Brahman is indescribable when a person sees himself not as a small being but as a part of the infinite universe, an immortal being.

Vedanta says that man can attain the feeling of immortality by being alive. This enlightenment frees man from the fear of death. Death is only an act/play of the infinite consciousness/ soul that is constantly changing its finite forms, and man ceases from suffering by attaching to the individual soul. This creation and destruction are understood to be a play in this infinite universe called the ever-changing Supreme Consciousness/Soul/Self.

An interesting question is raised in the Mundaka Upanishad: "What is that object by knowing which we know the nature of all objects in the universe?" After prolonged research, Indian philosophers came to know that by seeing our inner self, we are also made of that by which this entire infinite universe is made, and therefore our inner peace and happiness are characteristics of this infinite universe and every object in it. When the existence here is infinite, it is naturally peaceful and joyful. Also, there is no responsibility or duty for the infinite universe. That is why in the Bhagavad Gita, Lord Krishna says, "I have no responsibility in the three worlds, but I am engaged in intense activity/constant work/Karma." The inherent character of this created visible Universal Existence here is constant activity. So, we have to take it/understand it as it is. Because the infinite universe is the ultimate reality, there is nothing else to be compared with it in this universe because the existence here is infinite.

> **"Attach thyself not to; but equally attach" thyself not to stupid inactivity and suspension of All, whatever what you, are equal in all. conditions"**
>
> **– Vashista Geetha**

This Infinite Consciousness/Supreme Soul, the universe, is called "Sachidananda" (Bliss), the embodiment of *Sat + Chit + Ananda.*

Some people need meditation to reach this inner space within us and know its nature. The doubts about our aim of existence, birth, and death naturally torment a person constantly. This doubt can only be resolved through supreme knowledge. For this, the infinite essence must first be understood. The existence here is infinite. This world of phenomena has arisen in this infinity, and its existence is dependent on it. That is, it is indisputable that this entire infinite universe is the product of one infinite existence. "This universe was not created by an extra-cosmic God, nor is it the work of an outside genius. It is self-created, manifested, and self-destructed One infinite existence" - Swami Vivekananda. This is the secret of creation discovered by Indian philosophers.

However, it is not an easy task to understand the infinite universe as a single entity. For this, practising celibacy is needed means constantly paying attention to this principle until it is understood, and this final stage of understanding is said to be crossing the "river of Vaitarani" with great difficulty. The questions before Indian philosophers were about this secret of creation of God and the relationship between them. After many years of research and deep contemplation, the stage reached was *"Aham Brahmasmi"* means "I am Infinite consciousness". Thus, in an evolutionary process, dualism, special non-dualism, and finally non-dualism were reached by our philosophers. Dualism is the belief that the creator/God created this universe, and God remains separate from the Created Universe. Special non-dualism says that the Creator's element is also present in this universe. Advaita says that the Creator and this created infinite universe are not separate. Advaita proclaims the fact that there is no other second thing in this infinite universe, "*Sarvakhalvidam Brahma*". It should be said that reaching this peak of knowledge is a revolution of knowledge. There is no such thing as "*Paramatma Darshan*/Visiting the Infinite consciousness with the sharpest intelligence in any other religion of this world. Only Indian philosophers have spoken about this wonderful Paramatma Darshan/vision of Supreme consciousness. In the present time, only very few people are able to do this Darshan/Vision. There are various reasons for that. The teaching related to this was taught in a very ancient time in a manner and language suitable to the conditions of that time, and modern discoveries of science were not coordinated properly to make it understandable to this generation. In this present time, it is not much difficult to understand this philosophy when science is so advanced. Today, quantum physics has almost reached the conclusion that there is nothing in this infinite universe except "Pure Consciousness", as stated in Advaita philosophy. This was prophesied by Swami Vivekananda long ago.

Answer to Questions

How did this creation come into being? If there is a creator, where is the creator? Can we see that creator? Why did he create this? What is our ultimate duty in this creation? Does the soul remain after the death of a person? Is there rebirth? Many such questions arise within us. Finding satisfactory answers to these questions is a very difficult process at all times. Before seeking answers to these questions, we have to examine the origin of these questions. The origin of these questions is the events in this limited world in which we live, that is, we are deluded into finding the ultimate answers to the events in this limited world. For example, we see that there is a force and a cause for an event to happen, but in fact that cause, if we go to the source of the force that made it happen, all of them lose their existence in the ultimate sense. They become absorbed in infinity and become meaningless. That is, if we examine the questions that arise in us with the perspective of the Supreme Being, we will understand that they do not exist. The process of attributing the questions that arise in the finite world to the infinite philosophy is not correct because the events that occur here are not real and make us believe that they are real. In fact, it is not a correct perspective to think that the events that occur in the infinite existence should also provide answers to the questions that arise due to the events of the finite world. In fact, overcoming these questions with the perspective of the infinite Supreme Being is the biggest obstacle we have. If we can overcome this state, the principle of the infinite Supreme Being will be easily understood.

Scientists say that the cause of this expansion of the universe is 68 percent dark energy and 27% dark matter. We naturally want to understand how this creation came about. However, to find an answer to this, we need to shift our focus from the things we have observed in this limited world to the infinite universe. What does it mean to understand? It is nothing but comparison. I have observed certain phenomena/things in this finite world, so I have to say that the things related to this infinite universe should fit in with these. It is not correct to find answers about the infinite universe with reference to and comparing with limited finite worldly observations. The infinite reality/Existence here is beyond the realm/purview of Cause and effect. For Infinite existence, there cannot be a cause for its Existence; it is beyond the concept of Cause and effect. Our questions about the infinite universe like Why, how, when, and where lose their meaning when we start viewing this world from the viewpoint of Infinite Existence. When we think about creation, a new thing has come to light for us. Creation is a matter of a new thing being transformed from an old thing, but a completely new thing is not being created here. The concept of infinity is not so easy for us to understand because we have always been observing the limited world. But what is here is an infinite universe. When these planets, stars, living beings, energy, and sky that are called creation are seen in an infinite perspective, we get a new feeling and surprise. When we begin to understand this infinite principle, we come closer to the infinite Supreme Being, and in the final stage, we also attain enlightenment like a light, including the knowledge of our existence. This state is called Liberation, Moksha, *Kaivalyapadam, Paramapadam, and Parandamam.* As our scientific knowledge approaches the truth, new things start surprising us, as we observe the quantum of physics. Instead of looking for answers by attributing the things of the finite world to the infinite universe, we can understand the infinite existence very easily by accepting the infinite nature of existence. It is not possible for us to understand the infinite thing through our old method. Just as if we look at a one hundred square foot painting from a distance of one hundred centimetres, we would not be able to see the whole picture. The concept of infinity is beyond our imagination. But we can recognise that what is here is infinite through some kind of experience/feeling. That is, we should be able to see the truth of infinity as it is here, leaving the process of comparing it with our limited existence. When we start observing these mysteries of creation from the perspective of infinity, the understanding of the subject of transcendental knowledge becomes easier.

When new discoveries were emerging in modern science, people like Albert Einstein and Werner Heisenberg faced a very confusing situation because the truths that appeared before them seemed very different and revolutionary from the previous science.

It is natural for a human being not to immediately accept new things, whether it is an opinion or a scientific subject that has been discovered so far. It takes great intellectual power and courage to accept new things. Our ancestors gave us these scriptures with great love so that we could break free from these old beliefs, like a lion can break through a hunter's net, and gain infinite peace and happiness by understanding and experiencing this infinite principle. Unfortunately, in the present time, there are very few people who read these spiritual scriptures or talk about them.

Spiritual Freedom

"Physical freedom, mental freedom, and spiritual freedom" is the clarion call of the Upanishads.

In the present times, most of the people are just spiritual. What man needs is spiritual freedom. As part of that, we live in fear of God by worshipping idols. Indian spiritual knowledge of the Supreme Consciousness/Soul freed man from these fears and doubts thousands of years ago. That is, Indian philosophers, having gone beyond the realm of relative Existence (Karma Kanda) and reached the realm of knowledge (gnana Kanda) thousands of years ago, had the vision of the Supreme Consciousness. In the present time, only a very small number are able to use this knowledge and live a happy life. The majority are still far from this supreme knowledge and are unable to discover our priceless treasure trove of knowledge and make use of it.

Swami Vivekananda said:

"Each soul is potentially divine. The goal is to manifest this divinity by controlling nature, external and internal. Do this either by work, worship, psychic control, or philosophy - by one, more, or all of these - and be **Free.**"

This is the whole of religion. Doctrines, or dogmas, or rituals, or books, or temples, or forms, are but secondary details."

In the present era, man has to work continuously to improve his life by applying highly developed science and technology. After working hard until an adult age and earning enough for life, a doubt haunts him. Questions arise from time to time for answers about this creation, God, the purpose of his life, etc. Since the right answers are not found, those questions remain as painful doubts. Out of fear of God, people go to temples and seek refuge in various religious gurus. Some people may gain enlightenment due to these actions.

However, unfortunately, many people do not know that there is a treasure of knowledge that can solve their doubts in our ancient philosophy. There are also very few gurus who can guide us properly. In today's society with advanced science and technology, if we can properly bring before them the knowledge discussed and discovered in our Upanishads that has reached its ultimate level, it will be very easy to understand/realise Infinite consciousness.

I believe that modern-age intellectuals can easily understand this philosophy. Our situation is like our ancestors kept a great treasure in our house, and we did not know that it was there and did not benefit from it, suffering from poverty. Our ancestors wanted us all to experience such a great treasure of knowledge and spend our lives in peace and happiness. In this regard, the Westerners are more advanced than us in the creation of material wealth. It can be said that even to create wealth by probing the secrets of nature, scientists have to use their supernatural/imaginative power of knowledge. Sri Rama Thirtha once answered someone in America like this.

American question: Why do you think Indians are in such a poor state of poverty after having such a great wealth of knowledge?

Sri Ramatirtha: - Yes, you are right. We are talking about Vedanta. You are practising Vedanta.

That is, as Lord Krishna says at the end of the Bhagavad Gita, wherever this Vedic knowledge is practiced, there will certainly be wealth, knowledge, and righteousness.

For this pursuit of knowledge, today's educated intellectuals should directly read the Upanishads and Sri Bhagavad Gita, Sri Vasishta Gita, Sri Avaduta Gita, and Sri Ashtavakra Gita, and other Vedanta texts, investigate and try to understand them. If necessary, they can take advice and suggestions from such knowledgeable people in such an effort. People in the fields of science and technology naturally have a process of inquiry. The importance our ancestors gave to inquiry can be understood by looking at the verse in this Vasishta Gita. "It is through inquiry that the best men get intelligence, strength, energy, timely inspiration, action, and results of action, so such inquiry should always be engaged."

Just as we have created wealth and made our lives happy through human effort and inquiry, similarly, by taking a step further and contemplating on this infinite universe, we can surely attain supreme knowledge, attain the vision of the Supreme Consciousness, attain spiritual freedom, and experience eternal bliss.

Meditation

There are four types of yoga systems in the attainment of supreme knowledge: Karma, Bhakti, Raja, and Gnana Yoga. However, the final one is Gnana Yoga. Only through Gnana Yoga can a person attain perfect supreme knowledge and reach a higher state that is beyond worldly knowledge and see the Supreme Consciousness.

Meditation plays an important role in the system known as Raja Yoga. In the process of attaining supreme knowledge, the mind has to be controlled for concentration. After meditation becomes a habit, after some time, a person reaches a state of stillness, peace and bliss in the innermost state. This is the true nature of the Supreme Consciousness. To correctly recognise this state and to be constantly engaged in it, transcendental knowledge is very necessary. Every person experiences this state of stillness and bliss from time to time, but he does not know how to experience it continuously. The state of peace and bliss that exists between the flow of one thought and another is the true nature of the Supreme Consciousness. The work of the Vedanta Teachers is to teach us to recognise this state and experience it continuously.

Due to such a state, a person does not experience mental fatigue. He can perform daily activities with great power and wisdom without getting depressed from time to time.

After reaching the innermost state and establishing himself in a state where he cannot go any further deep within himself, the process of meditation stops. However, the ultimate goal of Brahman knowledge is to reach such a state unconsciously and experience happiness all the time. The stage of practice in this practice of knowledge is called the Brahmacharya stage. This is also the stage of the student. In this way, while one is in the pursuit of supreme knowledge, the mind is constantly fixed on the pursuit of Brahman knowledge without turning towards other worldly pleasures.

The ultimate goal of meditation is to attain such a state and then to rest in the ultimate state of peace and bliss constantly though not sitting in a meditative posture.

This state is called samadhi. That is, the state of being in a state of stillness and bliss, without allowing any influence to affect the inner world, looking at all events like gain and loss, hardship and happiness with equanimity. This is also called nirvikalpa samadhi. This is the direct and greatest benefit of transcendental knowledge.

Bhagavad Gita

Vasudeva sutam devam
Kamsa Chanura Mardhanam
Devaki paramanandam
Krishnam vande jagadgurum

When people were making wrong interpretations of Vedantic knowledge, the Supreme Lord Himself came to give the correct Vedanta interpretation, that is the Bhagavad Gita. That Supreme Soul is Shri Krishna.

> "Human race will never again see a brain as his who wrote Bhagavad Gita"
>
> – Swami Vivekananda

The thought of Shri Krishna standing alone giving the correct interpretation of Vedanta makes us afraid of it because we are creepers always waiting for the interpretations of others. Even today, very few people are studying and understanding Vedantic knowledge directly.

Regarding Vedanta knowledge, the Bhagavad Gita is a life-applying song. It teaches us how to apply this knowledge of Infinite consciousness and fight life's battle and get engaged in daily activities with the greatest enthusiasm, equanimity, and perfection.

First time in human history, Sri Krishna perfectly applied Vedanta knowledge/Brahma Jnana to people of all walks of life in the Bhagavad Gita. That's why Sri Krishna is called a great teacher of philosophy and also a perfect and complete incarnation of Supreme consciousness.

In the Bhagavad Gita, Lord Krishna especially taught Karma Yoga. That is, no human being can remain without performing work for a single moment. It is work that is necessary for earning a living or for the continuation of their life process itself. However, by giving more importance to the process of performing work and attaining the highest knowledge that leads to salvation, and thereby attaining salvation like the Yogis/Saints of knowledge, Lord Krishna has provided the great path and the gift of knowledge to all humanity.

Why Lord Krishna asked us to perform work without being attached to the fruits of work we can understand if we observe the truth that our ancestors discovered in the infinite universe.

> "That is infinite, this is infinite
> This infinity comes from infinity.
> From infinity, this infinity subtracted
> added to infinity remains infinity."

> – Isha Upanishad

This mean sum total entity of this infinite universe is constant without addition or subtraction eternally.

Since we are also in this existence, we should also do, that is, live or act as this infinite Universal creation works. If we once focus on the Infinite Consciousness and observe, this infinite universe is working for an infinite time, no new thing is added to it or taken away from it. Also, by working on this earth in our lives, we don't add any new matter here. What we are doing is changing the form of an object, in the production of food and mineral wealth from one form to another and shaping the external nature in a way that suits us and brings us happiness, that is, we are not removing a single new atom from this earth or adding it to this earth. Sri Krishna has advised us to abandon the results of work in the mind based on this truth. Abandoning the results of work does not mean abandoning the material wealth that is acquired by the results of work in the physical sense, but rather saying that we should not be attached to the results of our work internally in the mind and remain in peace and joy in the inner state without clinging to the results of work in the mind. It means saying that we should live happily in this world with detachment like a lotus leaf never attaches to drops of water. Without understanding this matter properly, people are unable to practice Karma Yoga as Sri Krishna has said and live a happy life. The Gita says that after working within the scope of intellect, we should immediately relax in the inner state of the Supreme Consciousness/Self/Soul.

Due to this process, the mind's peace, joy, and radiance are achieved. The mind gets immediate peace by sacrificing the results of work in the mind. Apart from this, for the first time, he declared that women and Shudras/working-class people were also eligible to gain spiritual knowledge, which was prohibited for them at that time. Because he had such a great heart, Lord Krishna is praised as the perfect incarnation even today. If other incarnations are revealed through various aspects of the Supreme Consciousness/Self/Soul, then the Bhagavatam says that Lord Krishna is the true Supreme Lord himself. Lord Krishna had iron muscles, steel nerves, a mind as hard as a diamond, the valour of a warrior and the radiance of Brahma Gnani. Swami Vivekananda advised everyone to live with these qualities. In today's society, there is a misconception that physical strength is the opposite of intelligence. In fact, only those who have good physical strength also have a good intellect. If we observe the scientists of today's Western countries, by eating good and strong food, they are able to unravel the great mysteries of nature in the fields of science and technology. That is lacking in today's Indian society. Strong intellect is found only in those who have a strong physical body.

In the practice of Karma Yoga, one has to get used to not having any association with the results of work in the mind. After doing any work, be it physical or mental, one should gradually learn through practice to relax in the state of the Supreme Consciousness/Soul within/above the intellect during the break. Then one can also do the work very skillfully. By always focusing on the results of work one cannot focus on the work being done. The fear that the result of the work will be against one's will reduces the energy and capabilities of a person. Therefore, one should do the work ahead without constantly thinking about the result. Because some circumstances may not be favourable, and the result may be against what was expected. It is possible to gather sufficient energy to try again and again through the detachment of results of work. After attaining enlightenment, Lord Krishna adopted the householder's life and became world-famous as a great Karma Yogi.

Shri Krishna first taught Karma Yoga in Vedanta to provide the knowledge of Brahman/Infinite consciousness, which provides supreme bliss to the working-class people. At that time, there was a perception that Brahman knowledge of Infinite consciousness was available only to those who adopted a monastic life. He refuted such a perception and explained in detail how those who work hard should also see the Supreme Consciousness. He said that in the practice of Karma Yoga, the main thing is to not be attached to the fruits of work in the slightest, but to fix the mind on the infinite Supreme Consciousness/Self and perform daily works because if you do not work, life is difficult and cannot sustain. Only a very small number of people can live without engaging in any productive activities, for example intellectuals, monks, and priests, but the majority of the population must necessarily produce goods through physical labour. In the Gita, he tells how one can reach the Supreme Consciousness/Self through non-attachment to the results of work while performing work. Since he helped all humans attain knowledge, even today, Lord Krishna is praised as the perfect incarnation and the Supreme Consciousness/Self. He exhorted that one should never allow weakness of heart to enter one's life. Working with great enthusiasm brings comfort in life and also the vision of the Supreme Consciousness/Self. Just as Arjuna, after gaining knowledge of the Supreme Consciousness/Soul, got rid of the doubt of what is right and what is wrong, and fought the war in Kurukshetra with great valour and became victorious, similarly, the message of the Gita is that everyone, after gaining knowledge of Infinite consciousness/Brahman, should live in this world without fear and sorrow.

Work with great enthusiasm in life and conquer enemies. Enjoying the pleasures of the world is the message of Sri Krishna in the Gita, as Swami Vivekananda has commented. In fact, Indians are currently lagging behind most of the countries of the world without fully following this.

The message of the Gita is to discard this body like an old garment when necessary without any fear. The message of the Gita is to live with such a sense of sacrifice and courage. Fear is sin according to Vedanta. The scientific way of thinking that does not allow for any superstitions is that of Lord Krishna. The objects made up of the five elements change their forms into other objects with time. If they give up their form, then if it is a living being, we consider it to be dead. If it is any object other than a living being, we say that the object is destroyed. The possibility of matter taking another form is more prevalent on planets like the Earth. A material transformation called living beings has taken place here due to the influence of minerals, air, water, and sunlight. Therefore, it is an illusion/mistake, according to Vedanta's knowledge, to think that there is a separate individual soul in every living being. We are mistaking ego as the individual soul. The ego is formed by the finite knowledge of the world one acquires from the environment in which one is raised and through education one gets. The ego completely belongs to the finite world and is a cause of many sufferings, so one has to cross the limited ego and realise the Infinite Consciousness/ego and merge in it and live peacefully and with bliss. According to Indian philosophy, there is no actual eternal existence for living beings in this creation. Only one infinite consciousness/self/soul, which can also be called the Supreme Consciousness/Self/Soul, has eternal existence. This infinite Supreme Consciousness/Self/Soul is the one who has created, maintained, and destroyed the innumerable worlds in the infinite universe since infinite time. That is, this infinite Consciousness experiences the world as a play within itself, like a dream.

So, Krishna says, "Wise never grieve either for people who are alive or dead." In the Bhagavad Gita, Lord Krishna also says that one can choose any path to see the infinite Consciousness, whether from the perspective of the subtle world/microscopic or from the perspective of the gross/macroscopic world.

Lord Krishna says that even if a person performs any work if he does not have an attachment/association with the result of his work according to his profession, he can attain the highest knowledge and see the Supreme Consciousness/Self/Soul. Now, without getting confused, one thing should be clearly understood. The fact that there is only one infinite Consciousness/self/soul here is also called the Supreme Consciousness/Self/Soul. Lord Krishna explained to Arjuna, through transcendental knowledge, the soul, birth and death, and no life after death, and made him action-oriented.

The inspiration for the Bhagavad Gita is said to be the Katha Upanishad. In the Katha Upanishad, a young devotee named Nachiketa waited for the king of death, Yama, at his doorstep without eating or sleeping for three days and nights. He impressed the king, Yama, with his attention and asked him about the origin of life and death, and got answers. Lord Yama explained that there is only One Infinite Consciousness/Self that exists here, and within it, all the visible Universes are created, manifested, and destroyed like a play.

Another important point made in the Gita is that the Supreme Knower/Spiritually Enlightened and the Supreme Consciousness/Soul are one,

"Four types of noble people worship me:

1. One who is in distress.

2. One who wants worldly pleasures.

3. One who has love/Bhakti on me and has longed for Knowledge of Infinite consciousness.

4. One who is Enlightened Spiritually. All the above four types of people are wise/noble, but the fourth one is one and the same with me, meaning He is Supreme consciousness itself (Paramatman himself)."

Sri Vasishtha also said the same thing.

"O Ramachandra, by acquiring the Supreme/Ultimate Knowledge of Infinite consciousness, man becomes the Supreme Consciousness/Self/Soul"

It would be beneficial if this ancient Indian philosophical knowledge was taught to children from an early age. Sri Vivekananda says to teach them with enthusiasm that the essence of philosophy is that you are the "infinite Ultimate consciousness/Self/Soul/*Thathvam Asi.*" Another unfortunate concept is prevalent in our society today. That is the misconception about those who are celebrated as avatars. Vedantic and other spiritual commentators say that avatars/ incarnations were born by some supernatural invisible force and lived in that way and displayed great qualities which are contrary to the teachings and way of life of incarnations and undermine the divinity of human nature. This kind of view undermines the very purpose of the teachings of great masters who taught practically following the knowledge they acquired and who wanted all humanity to follow the righteous path shown by them. This is nothing but alienating humanity from adopting the virtues of great people who are called Avataras/incarnations, which makes teachings of great masters not to be followed by people at large. But in reality, the truth is that they were all born as ordinary human beings, acquired Vedanta knowledge and did great deeds with that power of knowledge. "Never forget the glory of human nature. You are the greatest God ever present; all the avatars/incarnations are only waves on the infinite ocean which you are," says Sri Swami Vivekananda. Sri Krishna says this to the sage Utanga in the Mahabharata. "I will protect the Dharma/Righteousness by displaying the qualities of the beings in whom I incarnate."

In the present era, people study spiritual texts like the Bhagavad Gita at the age of retirement. This is not very useful.

"*Yoga karmasu kaushalam*" means to work skillfully and without attachment, says Lord Krishna.

A person who has acquired this knowledge can work with great power and abilities, free from many bondages and can be happy with a peaceful nature in the inner realm. Those who have acquired this knowledge can fill the society around them with peace, progress, and happiness.

Every action is accompanied by good and bad results. However, one should perform the action with an equal state of mind over both of these. For this, Shri Krishna Paramatma says a good thing in the Gita. There is another "*Ananda Paramatma Tattvam*", a blissful state within and above the senses, mind, and intellect. One should recognise this and make it a habit to spend time in it. That state is peaceful and joyful. A person who is engaged in action should make it a habit to go into that state and rest immediately after completing the action. This habit gradually becomes an eternal process, and he unconsciously reaches that state. Due to this, supreme peace and happiness come, and one also becomes healthier. Along with this, one should avoid thinking about the results of one's actions repeatedly. Because sometimes circumstances may not be favourable, and the results may be opposite to what we expected. So, one should set a goal of work and work without worrying much about the outcome of the action because worrying continuously about results will hinder the power and progress in the means of one's actions and disturb him internally too.

Those who have an even view of the results of actions are called *Sthitaprajna*. This state is also called *Samadhi*.

> **"Spirituality, the fire which burns up the straw of desire, is all that is meant by the word , not at all the attitude of silence and contemplation"**
>
> **– Vashista Geetha**

Instant Vision

We can directly see/experience this infinite existence. We can experience it in our minds. This is well explained in a verse in the Srimad Bhagavad Gita. The senses are higher than the objects that the senses perceive. Above the senses is the mind. Above the mind is the intellect. Above the intellect is the Infinite Consciousness Soul/Self. If we reach this state called the Infinite Consciousness/Soul/Self, we get immediate peace and joy. This is also explained in the Sri Vasishta Gita.

> **"The interval between the mind's passing from one idea to another—the period of calm between the two storms of Thought—may be described as the native condition of Self (Supreme Consciousness)"**
>
> **– Vasishta Gita**

Thus, directly seeing the infinite Supreme Consciousness/ Supreme Essence/Existence and experiencing joy is the immediate use and ultimate goal of this knowledge.

Self-application

After acquiring this transcendental knowledge about the Ultimate Infinite Consciousness, it is natural for a person to apply this knowledge to his existence immediately. As soon as he applies it to himself, a new flash of light immediately appears within him. When he realises that he is not a part of a limited mortal universe but a part of the immortal infinite universe, a new excitement shines. A person who has spent all his life in great doubt suddenly has his doubts dispelled and feels like he is floating in the infinite ocean with a broken bond. The mind gets peace. This gives him supreme happiness. He participates in his daily activities without being bound, like a play. The happiness that comes from the awareness that he is the infinite Supreme Consciousness/ Soul/Self cannot be achieved by any other material worldly pleasures.

Infinite Conscious Self

The subject of Infinite consciousness visualisation is the last stage of infinite Universal transcendental knowledge, but before experiencing or visiting it, one must fully understand transcendental knowledge. According to Indian philosophy, Soul/Self means the One infinite Self/soul, not individual Selves/souls. It is not correct to use the plural word Selves/souls. This is a very important point. This should be understood correctly. However, we also see many living souls/Selves in this creation. But, if we look at it from a transcendental perspective, we understand all living souls as different personifications/manifestations/reflections of the infinite Supreme Consciousness/Self/Soul. So here it is. The only infinite entity is this Supreme Consciousness/Self/Soul or Atma, as our ancestors, the great sages, have said. However, we can see this Supreme Consciousness/Soul/Self, which is called the Atma/Self within us, in the last stage of knowledge attainment. It is said in ancient Indian scriptures that this attainment of knowledge or the perfection of transcendental knowledge can be achieved through scientific study, inquiry, meditation, wisdom, or wisdom alone. Now, with the help of advanced science and technology, a modern man can very easily attain this knowledge and can immediately see the peaceful Infinite consciousness/Self/soul within himself in the intellect.

The characteristic of this infinite Supreme Self/Soul within us is described in this way in the Srivastava Gita. "The Supreme Self/Soul within us does not perish when the body is destroyed, does not grow when the body grows, does not move when the body is moved."

It is very surprising and interesting that the Infinite consciousness/Self/soul does not move when the body is moved. Since this infinitely pervading existence is in a still and permanent form and the Individual Self/Soul is in reality no other than it, it means that the Infinite Supreme Consciousness/Self/Soul within us does not move. If this matter is understood perfectly, it is like understanding the entire knowledge of infinite Universal Existence called Brahma gnana by Vedhanthins. The first and most important thing is that there is only one infinite Supreme Consciousness/Self/Soul, the so-called souls in the ultimate sense; there are no such things. After death, the body made of the five elements (Air, water, earth, fire and space) merges with the five elements, and then the existence of the Individual Self/soul ends with that. The question of reincarnation does not arise for the Individual Self/soul; that is, there is no rebirth. There is no need to fear rebirth. But the Infinite consciousness/Self/soul, which is infinitely present in every living being, in every object, and even in the sky, is constantly recreating such living beings made of the five elements and inanimate substances such as planets and stars. This does not mean that the individual soul in a person enters another living being. The five elements manifest in various forms in this infinite Supreme Consciousness/Self/Soul. The five elements can transform into other living beings or substances in another form. However, the individual soul's existence ends with a person's death. The matter of the individual soul leaving one body and taking another has become very confusing. The infinite Consciousness/Self creates various living beings through the five elements that it has within itself. After the death/destruction of a living being or an object, it transforms into another material form. This matter should be understood without any confusion. Only then can we properly understand the essence of the Geethas or Vedhantha, that is, the Vedanta/knowledge of Brahman. If possible, one should also study the Katha Upanishad. Similarly, one should also study the Vashita Gita. The true forms and essence of these living beings will be easily understood. As shown in movies, it is wrong to show that after death, a light flame goes up, leaving the dead body. Due to this, the original form and meaning of the infinite soul are misrepresented.

"*Atmavat Sarvabhutani*" The soul or the Supreme Infinite Consciousness/Self/Soul is present in all five elements: earth, water, fire, air, and sky.

Yoga

Yoga is connecting with God, that is the path of reaching God. This yoga has four branches. They are 1) Karma Yoga, 2) Bhakti Yoga, 3) Raja Yoga 4) Gnana Yoga; through the first three of the above, the fourth and last Gnana Yoga must be reached by which one attains salvation or the vision of the Supreme Self/Soul. To know more about Karma Yoga, one should study the Bhagavad Gita. According to Karma Yoga, if we can work continuously without being attached to the fruits of our actions internally/mentally, we can get closer to God. This is possible through practice. On the other hand, through Bhakti Yoga, if we strive with constant love and faith towards God, the intention to gain the ultimate knowledge can also be said about devotion. But in today's society, most people make devotion a business and offer gifts to God. They want God to give them what they ask for. This is not devotion but commerce/business. It is said that the greatest worship is to constantly keep the infinite Supreme Being in mind.

When it comes to Raja Yoga, the goal is to look within ourselves and discover our nature. For this, most people need to meditate.

"A fool goes to sleep and comes out as a fool, and a fool goes into meditation and comes out as an Enlightened one."

– Swami Vivekananda

Depending on their mental states, they see a stage in their inner self where no further progress can be made. That state is peaceful and joyful. This state is the true state of the infinite Supreme Being. Once a person reaches this state, he experiences that state repeatedly while acting in the external world. After some time, it becomes a habit to continuously spend time in that state of bliss, even while engaged in daily activities. In this way, being in such a state of bliss is called the greatest meditation. This kind of habit gives a person good health and radiance. Our intellect is in direct contact with the Supreme Self/Soul in a good and peaceful state of mind. A person with such a state of mind can also spread peace and happiness in the society around him. Only through the ultimate yoga of knowledge can the Supreme Self/Soul be seen. "There is no other way to salvation except knowledge."

I say, "– Sri Vasishta Gita"

"The wise man is my soul, the wise man and I are one and the same"

– Bhagavad Gita

There is a misconception that yoga is a limited process of practising physical yoga postures that give physical health and strength. This process is only a step in the practice of yoga. A healthy body is important to maintain a healthy mind/intellect, but only through the knowledge of the Supreme Self/Soul can the vision of the Supreme Consciousness/Soul be achieved. This complete process is called yoga. In the Gita, Sri Krishna advises Arjuna, "*Yogi Bhavo Arjuna.*" That is, the practice process adopted on the path of the vision of the Supreme Self/Soul is called yoga. It can be Karma, bhakti, raja, and Gnana Yoga. The ultimate goal of yoga is to practice one or two yogas or all of them together and finally have the darshan/vision/realisation of the Infinite Consciousness Self/Soul.

Formation of Character/Qualities

Every human has their own behaviour and life goals depending on their knowledge. For example, a person who deeply believes that there is a heaven and hell after this life spends their life practising the good deeds as far as possible suggested by elders so far to reach heaven after death also with a fear of going to hell after death. Similarly, a person who believes that this life is final and there is no other birth wants to experience as much as possible in this life. At the present time, a large number of people belong to this category. Since they are very selfish and violent and disturb peace in society, destroying the environment and using it for their own pleasures. Similarly, an Enlightened Spiritual man/Paramartha Gnani, who knows that the infinite existence here is eternal, that this creation, along with all living beings, is impermanent, lives in harmony with all of them without harming their fellow human beings or any other living being or the nature around them or the environment. Because such a person knows that every visible and invisible world here is filled with infinite pure consciousness, therefore, great knowledge is necessary for citizens with good qualities to exist in society. If the highest Paramatma/Paramartha knowledge is more common, it creates a great developed and peaceful society. The great people we see in history, be it in any field, science, social or political fields, are the people who have attained Paramartha knowledge/Highest ultimate knowledge, some on their own and some through their gurus. They are the ones who have reached the stage of great knowledge in society.

To act with great virtue and brilliance, the highest knowledge is necessary. Divine knowledge makes people of great virtue and selflessness. All the incarnate beings have attained divine knowledge and have great virtue and have guided society for ages, leading humanity on the path of progress.

The best example is the life of Sri Krishna, who, after gaining knowledge of Infinite Consciousness/Brahma gnana at the Ashram of Sage Sandipani in his teenage, fought throughout his life to protect and safeguard righteousness in society without caring for his life. That is why people take him as a model person even today, after more than five thousand years.

That is the power and effect of this Supreme knowledge on mankind.

Here another doubt arises. That is, the pride of a man who realises that this infinite universe is his true form increases, but what actually happens is that such a person does not have ego. Because once he transcends his limited ego and merges with this infinite universe, he becomes joyful/ blissful and without small ego. Therefore, a skilled dancer never makes a wrong step.

Quotations

Sri Dattatreya Avadhuta Gyani, who attained enlightenment at a young age, tried to explain Vedanta very clearly in his "Avadhuta Gita."

It is said that one can receive the knowledge of Brahman/infinite Universal Existence from any guru. He says that one should receive knowledge without looking at the guru, whether he is a boy, a monk, or a *sansari*. He says that one should not leave a diamond in the dust. He asks, should one not cross a river because a boat has no colour.

> "Never ask the past of a guru/Teacher. If you know the starting of a river, you would never drink a cup of water from it."
>
> – Swamy Chinmayananda

> "Vedas can't put injunctions to the Enlightened people because Vedas are nothing but recorded behaviour of such men"
>
> – Swamy Chinmayananda

"One should overcome the two egoistic processes
of renouncing or accepting this world and immerse
oneself in happiness because you are the infinite
Supreme Self/Soul"

– Avadhuta Gita

"Knowing that you are omnipresent, I want to go on pilgrimages and see you, and knowing that I cannot describe you in words, I describe you to people. Forgive me for these mistakes," says Sri Dattatreya. When this entire universe is filled with the eternal Supreme Self/Soul and I too am the same, who will prostrate to whom?

In the Avadhuta Gita, it is said that if the powerful tiger called the mind is brought under control, there is nothing in this universe that cannot be achieved. Everything in this universe is possible only because of the power of restraint.

"Everything in this world is achieved by freedom.
One will get physical, mental, and ultimately
spiritual freedom only by freedom."

– Ashtavakra Gita

"All growth ends in fading, all rising ends in falling, all meeting ends in parting; such indeed is the law of this world."

Liberation is not on the other side of the sky, nor in the netherworld, nor on earth; liberation lies in the mind purified by proper Spiritual Knowing.

Attach thyself not to Karma; but equally attach thyself not to stupid inactivity and suspension of all Karma, whatever you are, equal in all conditions.

The whole world is Spirit, there is nothing else in Reality;— Betake yourself to this view of things, and rest in peace, thus regaining your real Self.

There is no condition either of bondage or liberation; there is no duality and no unity; it is allbeing—out and out. This is the absolute truth.

Having destroyed sense with Sense; mind with Mind; egoism with Egoism; I stand supreme as the Self of all.

Spirituality, the fire which burns up the straw of desire, is all that is meant by the word Samadhi, not at all the attitude of silence and contemplation.

> The Supreme Lord, the one who dwells within the heart, is the main form. The form of Vishnu with the conch, the wheel, the mace, is the secondary one
>
> – Vashista Geeta

> People are prostrating before idols with ignorance about their real nature, which is ultimately infinite Existence, like a person searches for ghee (clarified butter) though having butter in his hand.
>
> – Yogi Vemana